WOMEN OF HOPE

AFRICAN AMERICANS WHO MADE A DIFFERENCE

JOYCE HANSEN

FOREWORD BY MOE FONER, EXECUTIVE DIRECTOR AND FOUNDER, BREAD AND ROSES CULTURAL PROJECT

SCHOLASTIC PRESS • NEW YORK

FOR MY MOTHER, LILLIAN HANSEN,

A WOMAN OF GRACE, GENEROSITY,

HUMILITY, AND STRENGTH. —J.H.

Text copyright © 1998 by Joyce Hansen
Foreword copyright © 1998 by Moe Foner
Photograph page 6: © Photographs and Prints, Schomburg Center for Research in Black Culture; photo by Oscar B. Willis • Photograph page 8: Amy Hill Hearth, "Having Our Say" © 1993; photo by Brian Douglas • Photograph page 10: Brian Lanker © 1993 • Photograph page 12: Charmian Reading © 1993 • Photograph page 14: Charmian Reading © 1993 • Photograph page 16: Chris Bennion © 1996 • Photograph page 18: Brian Lanker © 1993 • Photograph page 20: Brian Lanker © 1993 • Photograph page 22: Katherine Lambert © 1993 • Photograph page 24: Brian Lanker © 1993 • Photograph page 26: Brian Lanker © 1993 • Photograph page 28: National Aeronautics and Space Administration
Excerpt on page 18 from *And Still I Rise*, by Maya Angelou. Copyright © 1978 by the author.
Reprinted by permission of Random House.

LIBRARY OF CONGRESS CATALOGING-IN-PUBLICATION DATA
Hansen, Joyce.
Women of hope: African Americans who made a difference / by Joyce Hansen; foreword by Moe Foner.   p.   cm.
"Based on a series of posters entitled 'Women of Hope,' created by Bread and Roses Cultural Project, Inc." — T.p. verso.
Includes bibliographical references. Summary: Features photographs and biographies of thirteen African-American women, including Maya Angelou, Ruby Dee, and Alice Walker.
ISBN 0-590-93973-4
1. Afro-American women—Biography—Juvenile literature. 2. Afro-American women—Pictorial works—Juvenile literature. [1. Afro-Americans—Biography. 2. Women—Biography.] I. Bread and Roses Cultural Project II. Title.
E185.96.H27   1998   920.72'08996073—dc20   96-32117   CIP   AC

10 9 8 7 6 5 4 3 2 1   8 9/9 0/0 01 02 03

Printed in Mexico   49
First edition, November 1998

The display type was set in Copperplate 33bc. • The text type was set in Garamond 3.
Book design by Marijka Kostiw

This book is based on a series of posters entitled "Women of Hope," created by Bread and Roses Cultural Project, Inc.
For information regarding the poster series, please contact Bread and Roses Cultural Project, Inc., 330 West 42nd Street, Floor 7, New York, NY 10036 / 212-631-4565.

CONTENTS

FOREWORD

The striking photographs in this book were drawn from a series of posters honoring "Women of Hope." The posters were created by Bread and Roses, which is the cultural project of 1199 National Health and Human Services Employees Union, AFL-CIO. 1199 has had a long history of involvement in working for human and civil rights. Bread and Roses sprang from the belief that a union should also nourish the hearts and minds of members and their families.

The "Women of Hope" program is a major focus of Bread and Roses. Our members, who are mostly women of color, and their families, rarely see themselves reflected in role models portrayed in the media. We wanted our poster series to provide images of women, strong and courageous, inspired to fight against injustice in ways they knew how. Through their poems and stories and many achievements, they inspire us to live and work in ways that help shape a fairer world.

Our goal is to honor courageous, creative women of color whose persistence and vision gave society hopefulness and inspiration — an inspiration we still seek today.

Choosing which women to profile here was difficult, but we finally selected these thirteen from hundreds of names submitted to us by friends and advisers all over the country.

When the posters were issued, we were touched by how they found their way into the hearts of people everywhere, young and old; people who wanted the images of these women nearby. Now they are present in homes, in thousands of schools, libraries, community centers, government offices, and religious organizations. They are on subway platforms, bus shelters, trains, and in airports. Wherever they are, pictures of these indomitable women lend a presence of strength and hope.

We hope this book will provide yet another platform for young people who are desperately in need of role models to serve as guides for living productive and meaningful lives.

As Gloria Steinem has said: "*Women of Hope* will inspire all Americans, especially our youth, who have been denied the knowledge that greatness looks like them."

MOE FONER

EXECUTIVE DIRECTOR AND FOUNDER

BREAD AND ROSES CULTURAL PROJECT

"WE PLEAD NOT FOR
THE COLORED PEOPLE ALONE,
BUT FOR ALL VICTIMS . . . "

IDA B. WELLS-BARNETT
BORN JULY 16, 1862, HOLLY SPRINGS, MISSISSIPPI ● DIED MARCH 25, 1931

"I was only fourteen years old. After being a happy, light-hearted schoolgirl I suddenly found myself at the head of a family," Ida B. Wells-Barnett said in her autobiography.

Born into the turbulent times of slavery and the Civil War, Ida B. Wells was destined to become a fearless, insistent voice speaking out against injustice. Her determined spirit and selfless dedication to others was evident at an early age — particularly at a time when tragedy struck her family.

When her parents died in the yellow fever epidemic in 1878, various neighbors in her community offered to take in the six children. But Ida, who was the eldest, refused to separate her family. Instead, she lengthened her skirts to make herself look older and obtained a teaching position in a rural school. First her grandmother, then a friend of her parents watched the children while Ida worked to support them and herself.

It was Ida's mother and father, who had both been enslaved, who gave her the self-confidence, strength, and determination to triumph over adversity. "Our job was to go to school and learn all that we could," Ida once said, describing her childhood.

By 1884, Ida moved to Memphis, Tennessee, where she secured a better teaching position. It was there where she fought the first of many battles against segregation and unjust laws that denied African Americans the same civil rights as other citizens. She filed a lawsuit against a railroad company when a conductor tried to drag her from the comfortable ladies' car of the train to the packed, segregated smokers' car. African Americans were not allowed to sit in any other part of the train. Though she lost the lawsuit, she wrote an article about the incident, and her career in journalism was launched. The article was reprinted in many black publications, and Ida discovered that her words moved people and stirred them to action. She purchased part ownership in a newspaper she called *Free Speech*. In 1891, she wrote about the inferior education that black children in Memphis were receiving in their segregated schools. Her articles were so revealing, she lost her teaching job. However, instead of being silenced, she passionately continued her work on the newspaper.

On March 9, 1892, when three black men were lynched (killed by a mob) because their successful grocery store in a black neighborhood drew customers away from a white-owned store, Wells-Barnett was outraged. Once again she used her pen like a powerful sword. Through a series of scathing articles, publications, and speeches in America and England, she exposed the terror of the many lynching incidents in the southern states. In May 1892, her inflammatory editorial on lynching was published in *Free Speech*. When a mob of angry whites threatened her life, she moved to Chicago where she continued to speak out against mob rule and to fight for social change until her death.

The brave, determined girl, who kept her family together, did not wait for the world to change. Instead, she changed the world around her.

"THE FAMILY MOTTO WAS,

'YOUR JOB IS TO HELP SOMEBODY.'"

THE DELANY SISTERS

ANNIE ELIZABETH (BESSIE) DELANY (LEFT)
BORN SEPTEMBER 3, 1891, RALEIGH, NORTH CAROLINA • DIED SEPTEMBER 25, 1995

SARAH (SADIE) LOUISE DELANY (RIGHT)
BORN SEPTEMBER 19, 1889, LYNCH'S STATION, VIRGINIA

"**B**essie and I have been together since time began, or so it seems. Bessie is my little sister, only she's not so little. She is 101 years old, and I am 103," Sadie Delany once said.

The Delanys were a remarkable family. Their father, born into slavery in 1858, rose to become the first African American to hold the position of bishop of the Episcopal Church. The ten Delany children were raised in a protected environment on the campus of the Saint Augustine's School in Raleigh. It was a school for black students, where their father was the priest and vice principal.

"We had a blessed childhood, which was unusual in those days for colored children," the sisters recalled.

"Your job is to help somebody," was the family motto, and the sisters never forgot that. Working all of their lives in "helping professions," they both taught in North Carolina once they finished their own secondary schooling. They wanted to continue their education. But because they were African American, none of the southern universities offering advanced degrees would accept them.

Even though Sadie would have preferred to stay and help her people in North Carolina, they saved their money and joined the great migration of African Americans who left the South for jobs and advantages in the northern cities. "I'd just have to help my people up *there*," Sadie said.

The sisters moved to Harlem, in New York City, and attended Columbia University. There Sadie earned a bachelor of science degree in 1920, and a master's degree in education in 1925. Bessie earned a doctorate of dental surgery in 1923. This was quite an accomplishment at a time when few Americans, black or white, went beyond high school.

Sadie Delany became the first black home economics teacher in a New York City high school. Bessie became the second black woman to be licensed to practice dentistry in New York.

Always living the family motto,"Dr. Bessie" — as her patients called her — said, "I never turned anyone away because they couldn't pay me." She practiced dentistry in Harlem for twenty-seven years.

The Delany sisters were like living history books. Born at a time when slavery and the Civil War were still fresh memories for many Americans, they lived long enough to see Rosa Parks, Fannie Lou Hamer, Dr. Martin Luther King, Jr., and the end of the Jim Crow laws that kept them from attending a university in the South.

Their lives have been a testament to the importance of education, self-esteem, discipline, and a generous spirit.

"There was a former slave who lived alone," the sisters said of their growing up years. "Mama always sent us over there to check up on him. Every Sunday, we shared our dessert with him. . . ." Throughout their long lives, they never stopped sharing.

"THE ONLY THING THAT IS

REALLY WORTHWHILE IS

CHANGE — AND IT'S COMING."

SEPTIMA POINSETTE CLARK

BORN MAY 3, 1898, CHARLESTON, SOUTH CAROLINA • DIED DECEMBER 15, 1987

All of her life, Septima Clark was an agent for change. The amazing woman and teacher that Septima became emerged amid the creeks, sandy roads, and poverty of Johns Island, South Carolina.

When Septima graduated in 1916 from Avery Normal Institute, a black private school in Charleston, she accepted a teaching position in a small rural school on Johns Island. At only eighteen years old, she was both principal and teacher in a two-room schoolhouse. There was only one other teacher to help with the 132 students.

The students had spent more hours working in the fields than sitting in a classroom, and the school itself had no resources. But Septima Clark met the challenge.

"We had benches without backs, and they knelt on the floor to do their writing, and put the pages on top of the bench. . . .

"We had no blackboards . . . I wrote their stories . . . of their country right around them, where they walked to come to school, the things that grew around them. . . . They told them to me, and I wrote them on dry cleaners' bags and tacked them on the wall. . . . It's surprising that I had so many children who became very competent."

Miss Seppie, as the islanders called her, also held adult classes in the evening. Septima taught on the island for three years before returning to Charleston, where she was offered a new teaching position.

In Charleston, she began what would become a life devoted to challenging segregation and the illiteracy it fostered. She joined other African-American teachers and successfully petitioned the South Carolina legislature to pay black teachers the same wages as white teachers and to allow black instructors to teach in the Charleston public schools. Up to that time, African Americans could teach only in private schools in Charleston or in rural areas like Johns Island.

Then, in 1956, this dedicated teacher met the greatest challenge of her life when she refused to give up her membership in the National Association for the Advancement of Colored People (NAACP), one of the oldest civil rights organizations in the nation. She lost the teaching license she'd held for forty years, along with her pension. Southern states and local governments retaliated against blacks who tried to change the system.

However, this courageous master teacher would not be moved. In 1961, she joined Martin Luther King, Jr., and the Southern Christian Leadership Conference (SCLC) and continued her fight for equality.

As she traveled throughout the South, Clark designed reading and writing courses and trained teachers to run citizenship schools, known as Freedom Schools. The schools helped thousands of people exercise their right to vote.

She eventually settled again in her Charleston home and, after long legal battles with the State of South Carolina, received her pension and back pay. She stood up for her rights and was vindicated: In 1982, she received the Order of the Palmetto, which is South Carolina's highest honor for outstanding service to the state.

To young people she said, "I'd tell the children of the future that they have to stand up for their rights . . . they need to come forth and stand up for some of the things that are right."

"PEOPLE HAVE TO BE MADE TO UNDERSTAND THAT THEY CANNOT LOOK FOR SALVATION ANYWHERE BUT TO THEMSELVES."

ELLA JOSEPHINE BAKER

BORN DECEMBER 13, 1903, NORFOLK, VIRGINIA • DIED DECEMBER 13, 1986

Ella Baker was an unsung heroine, and a powerful woman behind the men who led the civil rights movement of the 1950s and 1960s. She sought no glory for herself as she went about the business of lending her incredible organizational skills to foster justice, equality, and democracy.

The values that shaped her thinking were formed in the small black southern community of Littleton, North Carolina, where she was raised by her grandparents. She learned from her grandfather, a minister and respected leader, the importance of self-help and of aiding those who are in need.

In 1929, two years after graduating from Shaw University in Raleigh, North Carolina, at the top of her class, she moved to Harlem in New York City. The Depression brought unemployment and poverty to many Americans, and here, Ella found the work that would absorb her for the rest of her life: political activity.

Beginning in 1930 with a club to help poor people stretch their money by sharing what they had, Baker spent the next fifty years organizing and guiding people and movements. She was a major force in the National Association for the Advancement of Colored People (NAACP), serving as field secretary, national director of branches, and president of the New York City chapter.

When Dr. Martin Luther King, Jr., sought her assistance to organize the Southern Christian Leadership Conference (SCLC) headquarters and activities, Ella Baker brought to the SCLC twenty years of organizational experience. In her work with Dr. King and the SCLC, she stressed her belief that ordinary people must be involved in political activity. "Strong people do not need strong leaders," she once said.

In 1960, when students across the South began to conduct sit-ins, sitting at lunch counters and other public places where African Americans were not allowed, the Student Nonviolent Coordinating Committee (SNCC) was born. They, too, sought her help. Guided by Baker's wisdom and experience, African-American students organized one of the largest student movements in United States' history.

She was honored with the name *Fundi*, a Swahili word for a person who passes skills and knowledge to a younger generation.

Baker continued to work as an adviser and consultant to nearly fifty organizations and coalitions over the course of her life. She did not seek a leadership role; instead, she unselfishly created leaders. Ella Baker never lost sight of the important goals of the social movements she helped to fashion — democracy, equality, and justice for all people.

"I AM SICK AND TIRED

OF BEING SICK AND TIRED.

WE MUST STAND UP FOR OUR FREEDOM."

FANNIE LOU HAMER

BORN OCTOBER 6, 1917, MONTGOMERY COUNTY, MISSISSIPPI • DIED MARCH 14, 1977

When Fannie Lou Hamer was six years old, she began working in the cotton fields with her mother, her father, and her twenty older brothers and sisters. Like other children in Sunflower County, Mississippi, she received some early schooling. However, the cycles of working cotton shaped her days, and everything else came second.

"I used to watch my mother with tears in my eyes," Hamer said. "I used to see my mother cut those same trees with an ax just like a man. . . . She would carry us out in these areas . . . and we would have to rake up the brush. . . and burn it."

As Hamer grew, anger over their oppression burned in her heart like the leaves and the brush. She once told the owner of the plantation where she worked, " . . . our people go to the army just like your white people go . . . and then when they come back home, if they say anything, they killed, they lynched. . . . "

In the summer of 1962, when the students from the Student Nonviolent Coordinating Committee (SNCC) came to Sunflower County, Mississippi, to register African Americans to vote, she felt that this was the event she had been waiting for all her life.

Hamer said, "I didn't know that black people had the right to register to vote." Because of unfair literacy tests and impossibly high poll taxes (tax payment in order to vote), poor sharecropping families like the Hamers could not vote.

Fannie listened to what the young people had to say about the rights of African-American citizens. But when she did register to vote, the wrath of the white men who owned the farms and plantations where the black sharecroppers worked fell on her. Hamer was fired from her job as timekeeper on one of the plantations, and her life was threatened. She was forced to leave her family and stay with friends. When a group of whites shot into the house where she stayed, she left the county for a few months. But Hamer would not be frightened off the road to freedom she'd begun to travel.

She joined SNCC and when she began to register other blacks, she was arrested and beaten unmercifully. The beatings did not deter this brave and deeply religious woman, who often began her speeches with the song "This Little Light of Mine."

In 1964, she helped found the Mississippi Freedom Democratic Party and captured the attention of the nation when she stood before the Democratic National Convention and said, "If the Freedom Democratic Party is not seated now, I question America."

She worked tirelessly for the poor and underprivileged, no matter what race. In 1969, she helped found the Freedom Farm Cooperative, and one of the first families the cooperative aided was a poor white family. Hamer recognized the suffering of all poor people. She said, "We have a job as black women, to support whatever is right." Her light still shines.

"THAT'S WHAT BEING YOUNG IS ALL ABOUT.

YOU HAVE THE COURAGE AND THE DARING

TO THINK THAT YOU CAN MAKE A DIFFERENCE."

RUBY DEE

BORN OCTOBER 27, 1924, CLEVELAND, OHIO

The direction Ruby Dee's life would take was apparent, even when she was a young student. She cared about social issues, loved language, and was comfortable speaking in front of an audience.

Ruby's first introduction to literature, music, art, and poetry came from her family, who moved to Harlem, in New York City, when she was an infant. Her mother was a teacher and exposed her children to the arts. "I love language and authors and music and how they can all interconnect," Ruby has said.

Ruby Dee majored in French and Spanish at New York City's Hunter College. She also studied acting and joined the American Negro Theater (ANT) in Harlem.

In 1943, when Ruby Dee made her Broadway debut in *South Pacific*, it was just a small walk-on role. But it was the first step in a long and distinguished acting career.

Ruby's decision to seriously pursue acting was a brave one indeed, for in 1946, when she starred in her first major Broadway play, *Anna Lucasta*, there were few good dramatic roles for black actors. They were often relegated to playing either comic characters or servants.

When the ANT production of *Anna Lucasta* appeared on Broadway, theatergoers and critics all over the country noticed what black actors had always known, that African-American actors could play a wide range of roles.

In 1946, she appeared in the play *Jeb*, about the racism that black World War II soldiers faced when they returned home to America after the war. Her future husband, actor and playwright Ossie Davis, starred in the title role. This combination of relevant social issues with dramatic art would be the hallmark of Ms. Dee's career. Appearing in her first film in 1946, *Love in Syncopation*, she went on to perform roles as varied as baseball great Jackie Robinson's wife in *The Jackie Robinson Story*, and Mary Tyrone in Eugene O'Neill's *Long Day's Journey into Night*. She has also portrayed Harriet Tubman and appeared in *The World of Sholem Aleichem*. She starred in both the stage and film versions of the 1959 play *A Raisin in the Sun* by Lorraine Hansberry. And in 1961, she played Lutiebelle in *Purlie Victorious*, written by Ossie Davis. In 1965, she continued to break through racial barriers by becoming the first black actress to appear in lead roles at the American Shakespeare Festival. She won a Drama Desk Award for her performance in the play *The Wedding Band*. She also won the prestigious Obie Award in 1971 for her performance in another play, *Boesman and Lena*. She has appeared in many films, among them *Buck and the Preacher* and *Black Girl*.

Ms. Dee's career has spanned generations. She is now known to younger audiences through the television miniseries *Roots: The Next Generation*, and Spike Lee's films *Do the Right Thing* and *Jungle Fever*. She was inducted into the Theater Hall of Fame in 1988, and in 1991 won an Emmy for Best Supporting Actress in *Decoration Day*.

Ruby Dee shunned demeaning roles, even when few parts were available to a black actress. She courageously spoke out on many social issues, even when it hurt her career. Her life and her work set a shining example of how integrity and pride are essential ingredients for a successful life.

YOU MAY WRITE ME DOWN IN HISTORY

WITH YOUR BITTER, TWISTED LIES,

YOU MAY TROD ME IN THE VERY DIRT

BUT STILL LIKE DUST, I'LL RISE.

MAYA ANGELOU

BORN APRIL 4, 1928, ST. LOUIS, MISSOURI

"**I** was mute for five years," Maya Angelou has said. "I wasn't cute and I didn't speak. . . . But my grandma told me all the time, 'Sister, Mama don't care what these people say about you being a moron, being a idiot. Mama don't care. Mama know, Sister, when you and the good Lord get ready, you're gonna be a preacher.'"

In *I Know Why the Caged Bird Sings*, the first of her five autobiographies, Maya Angelou begins to chronicle her life. She was a little girl with a poet's heart. But when she was seven, her song was silenced by a terrible experience and she stopped speaking. With the help of her grandmother who raised her in Stamps, Arkansas, the close-knit black community there, and a perceptive teacher who recognized her literary gifts and introduced her to literature, Maya found her voice again. She graduated from her segregated school at the top of her eighth-grade class.

She left Arkansas at thirteen to go to California to live with her mother. By sixteen, she had a child of her own to raise. "The greatest gift I've ever had was the birth of my son. . . . When he was small, I knew more than he did, I expected to be his teacher. So because of him I educated myself. When he was four . . . I taught him to read. But then he'd ask questions, and I didn't have the answers, so I started my lifelong love affair with libraries. . . . "

She also refused to be controlled by a society that defined her as inferior because she was black and female.

"I decided many years ago to invent myself. I had obviously been invented by someone else — by a whole society — and I didn't like their invention." Maya Angelou redefined herself. When she was in her twenties, she studied dance and was in a musical that toured Europe and Africa. Angelou also used her talents to try to help make the world a better place. In 1960, she and another performer wrote, produced, and appeared in the revue *Cabaret for Freedom* to raise money for the civil rights movement. She also spent time in Ghana, West Africa, working as a journalist in the 1960s. She has written, produced, directed, and acted in theater, movie, and television productions. She was nominated for an Emmy Award for her performance in the television miniseries *Roots* and was nominated for the Pulitzer prize in poetry. Maya Angelou also has twelve honorary doctorates.

Millions of Americans saw and heard her recite her poem "On the Pulse of Morning" for President Clinton's inauguration in 1993.

The message she brings through the example of her life and her art is clear. "All of my work is meant to say, you may encounter many defeats, but you must not be defeated."

Maya Angelou continues to rise, and we soar with her.

19

"MY WORLD DID NOT SHRINK BECAUSE

I WAS A BLACK FEMALE WRITER.

IT JUST GOT BIGGER."

TONI MORRISON

BORN FEBRUARY 18, 1931, LORAIN, OHIO

Toni Morrison, born Chloe Anthony Wofford, is one of the most celebrated and successful writers in the United States.

When she was growing up, Morrison's parents passed on to their children the rich African-American oral tradition of folktales, Br'er Rabbit stories, stories about Africans who could fly, ghost stories, humor, the rhythms and resonance of African-American language and music. All of these elements found their way into Morrison's novels.

Toni Morrison's parents also introduced their children to the written word. Toni could read by the time she entered the first grade. When she was only a teenager, she read the famous Russian and English classics, which also influenced her future work.

She graduated from high school with honors and entered Howard University in Washington, D.C., where she graduated with a degree in English. She went on to earn a master's degree in English at Cornell University in 1955.

Though she taught college, married, and began to raise a family, writing was always an important part of her life. By 1964, she was a divorced, single mother with two sons. She worked as a textbook editor during the day and wrote at night.

Morrison's first novel, *The Bluest Eye*, is set in her hometown of Lorain, Ohio, and tells on one level the deceptively simple story of a black girl who thinks that if she has blond hair and blue eyes, she will be accepted and loved. Toni Morrison, however, through her evocative use of language and imagery, is actually telling a complex tale of race, the clash of cultures, and the resulting damage to the psyche of a young girl.

Toni Morrison went on to write six other highly acclaimed novels that reach the heart of the African-American experience in all of its varied facets. "When I wrote *Sula*," Morrison said of her second novel, "I knew I was going to write a book about good and evil and about friendship."

The books that followed — *Song of Solomon*, 1977; *Tar Baby*, 1981; *Beloved*, 1987; *Jazz*, 1992; and *Paradise*, 1998 — explore the history, culture, mythology, and folklore of African Americans in ways that touch us all. "The problem I face as a writer is to make my stories mean something . . . I want my books to always be about something that is important to me, and the subjects that are important in the world are the same ones that have always been important."

Toni Morrison has won some of the most prestigious awards given to writers, including the Pulitzer prize for her novel *Beloved* in 1988, and the Nobel prize in literature in 1993.

Morrison continues to write, lecture, and teach. She has been a distinguished professor at several universities and has received ten honorary degrees.

"Writing wonderful books is not going to make me a wonderful person," she says. "I alone can improve myself and make myself more like the person I would like to grow to be."

"SERVICE IS THE RENT
WE PAY FOR LIVING."

MARIAN WRIGHT EDELMAN
BORN JUNE 6, 1939, BENNETTSVILLE, SOUTH CAROLINA

When Marian Wright Edelman was growing up in Bennettsville, South Carolina, during the 1940s and 1950s, she couldn't play in the public playgrounds or sit at drugstore lunch counters and order a Coke — because she was African American, and Bennettsville was segregated.

Blacks could not use the town's public facilities, such as its parks, playgrounds, or restaurants, so Marian's minister father built a playground and a small cafeteria behind his church for his own and other black children in the segregated community. "Whenever he saw a need, he tried to respond," Marian says of her father. And Marian Wright Edelman followed in his footsteps.

Influenced by the black southern community where she was born and raised, Edelman has taken the moral and cultural values she received as a child and used them to change the lives of children everywhere.

"The adults in our churches and community made children feel valued and important. They took time and paid attention to us. We were told that the world had a lot of problems; that black people had an extra lot of problems . . . but that being poor was no excuse for not achieving." She was also taught that she had a responsibility to help those less fortunate than herself.

During her years at Spelman College, Edelman was actively involved in the civil rights movement. And after graduating from Yale University Law School, she became the first black woman to pass the bar exam in Mississippi. She also worked for the National Association for the Advancement of Colored People (NAACP), helping students who had been jailed for holding sit-ins and other demonstrations.

Edelman's upbringing, which stressed the importance of service to her community, no doubt influenced her decision to offer her services to an even larger community. Like her father, she stepped in where she saw a need. One of the greatest areas of need she found was with America's many poor children. They had no one to speak out on their behalf — no one to make sure that there were laws and government policies in place to protect them.

In 1968, she moved to Washington, D.C. Her work there, and later on in Boston, led her to organize the Children's Defense Fund in 1973, which has successfully made Americans aware of the problems and issues that affect the health and well-being of children all over the country. The goal of the Children's Defense Fund is to show the American nation that it must invest money and resources to protect and aid children. Marian Wright Edelman has been called one of the most effective supporters of poor children and their families.

She has received thirty honorary degrees and the highly prestigious MacArthur Fellowship. She has also written several books: *Children Out of School in America*, *Portrait of Inequality*, and *The Measure of Our Success*.

Marian Wright Edelman says, ". . . the legacy I want to leave is a child-care system that says no kid is going to be left alone or unsafe."

"IT'S SO CLEAR THAT YOU HAVE TO CHERISH EVERYONE . . . EVERY SOUL IS TO BE CHERISHED . . . EVERY FLOWER IS TO BLOOM."

ALICE WALKER
BORN FEBRUARY 8, 1944, EATONTON, GEORGIA

Alice Walker is the youngest of eight children in a Georgia sharecropper family. When she was eight years old, one of her brothers accidentally shot her in the eye with a BB gun. She lost sight in that eye and, with her confidence shaken, she withdrew into herself.

"For a long time I thought I was very ugly and disfigured. This made me shy and timid." It was at this point that she read stories and began to write poems. Reading and writing became her way of escaping the harsh southern rural life around her. "I can recall that I hated it, generally. The hard work in the fields, the shabby houses, the evil, greedy men who worked my father to death and almost broke the courage of that strong woman, my mother."

As valedictorian of her high school graduating class, she earned a scholarship from the state of Georgia. With the scholarship and a seventy-five-dollar donation from the struggling farm families in her community, Walker entered Spelman College in Atlanta. She then went on to Sarah Lawrence College in New York, where she graduated in 1965.

Alice Walker returned to the South, where she became actively involved in the civil rights movement, while continuing to write. Her first collection of poetry was published in 1968. In 1970, she published her first novel, *The Third Life of Grange Copeland*, a story set in the rural South, a landscape she knows well. The novel focuses on the brutal and bitter relationship between a husband and wife, trapped by generations of racism, poverty, and ignorance. Her second novel, *Meridian*, explores her own generation and the impact of the civil rights movement. Her third novel, *The Color Purple*, which was her most celebrated, won the Pulitzer prize in fiction and the American Book Award in 1983. This novel was also made into a major motion picture.

The Color Purple is told through a series of letters written by a young, abused girl to her sister and to God. Also set in the rural South, the novel gives voice to the pain of all women who have been made to feel that their lives are of no value.

Alice Walker continues to explore social issues in her writing, especially the problems and concerns of women worldwide. She has never forgotten, though, the place and the people who first inspired her stories and poetry.

In one of her essays she wrote lovingly about her mother. "Because of her creativity with her flowers, even my memories of poverty are seen through . . . sunflowers, petunias, roses . . . I notice that it is only when my mother is working on her flowers that she is radiant. . . . She is involved in work her soul must have. . . .

"Guided by my heritage of a love of beauty and a respect for strength — in search of my mother's garden, I found my own."

"THE CIVIL RIGHTS MOVEMENT MADE MANY THINGS POSSIBLE WHICH WOULD NOT OTHERWISE HAVE BEEN POSSIBLE."

ALEXA CANADY
BORN NOVEMBER 7, 1950, LANSING, MICHIGAN

Alexa Canady and her brother were the only black students in their local elementary school. Alexa says that when she took the second-grade California reading test, her scores were so high that one of the teachers lied about which scores were Alexa's. The teacher was fired. "The teacher thought it was inappropriate for me to have done that well," Alexa said.

Dr. Alexa Canady has "done well" ever since, excelling in spite of those who would deny that she was intellectually gifted because she was black and female. "Racism was always presented to me as their problem and not our problem." Refusing to allow stereotypes of women and blacks to stop her, Dr. Canady completed medical school, has taught medicine at several large universities and, in 1981, at thirty years of age, she became the first black woman neurosurgeon in the United States.

Dr. Canady recalls that when she was a child she knew many educated African Americans who could not get professional jobs that matched their qualifications. Alexa was aware when she graduated from college that she needed more than good grades to reach her goals.

She says that political activity is still necessary to insure that people are treated fairly. "When I got a residency in neurosurgery, I got it not because I'm smarter than somebody forty years ago, but because the politics were such that they needed a black woman and I was there and qualified."

Dr. Canady has not been afraid to follow her own heart and mind. She switched her major in college from mathematics to science because math didn't excite her. She completed her internship and residency at the University of Michigan instead of remaining an intern at Yale Medical School as her parents advised. She felt that the midwestern school was better for her.

Dr. Canady also believes in taking risks. Even though she had excellent grades and credentials when she left medical school, people were shocked that she would want to be a neurosurgeon. She felt that they were really saying, "How can you, a black woman, have the audacity to want to do this?"

Dr. Canady says that you must really love what you are doing. "I felt at home in neurosurgery. I couldn't play it nice and safe because that wasn't me." Dr. Alexa Canady loves her work, and says that her job is not to cut, but to help people, ". . . which often includes cutting. . . . You get to be a part of people's families. . . .You get to see the strengths of the human spirit that can survive terrible . . . things."

To young people she says, "It's your vision; it's your life; it's yours to make happen."

"Don't be limited by others' limited imaginations."

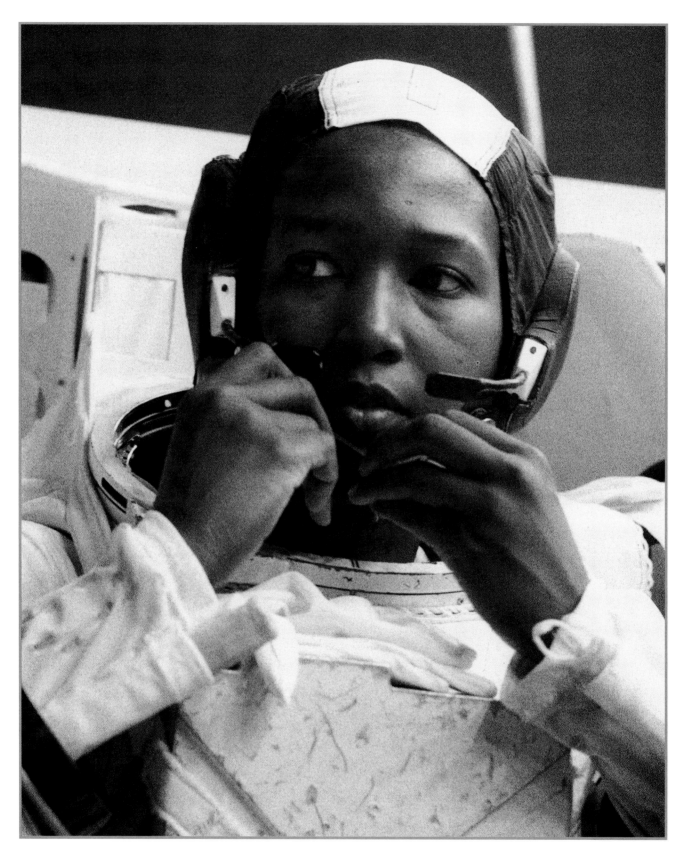

Mae C. Jemison

Born October 17, 1956, Decatur, Alabama

Mae Jemison was only in kindergarten when she told her teacher she wanted to become a scientist.

"You mean a nurse," the teacher responded. But Mae Jemison knew that she wanted to be a scientist, a dream her teacher thought was impossible. How could a girl — especially an African-American girl — hope to become a scientist?

Mae had another dream, too. After seeing launches of the *Mercury* and *Gemini* program flights on television, space exploration fascinated her. "I thought of myself as just being in space and looking around and doing whatever it is that astronauts do . . . I definitely had fantasies of being on another planet or on the moon," she says.

"I've wanted to be involved in the astronaut program since I was a child. I never have had any question I could do it." Mae Jemison had enough confidence in herself to make her dream come true. She remained focused on her goal — to become a scientist, while never forgetting her dream — to become an astronaut.

Using her intellectual gifts and abilities and following the example of her hardworking parents, Mae Jemison completed high school in Chicago in only three years, entered Stanford University at sixteen, and graduated with a bachelor of science in chemical engineering. She also fulfilled requirements for a bachelor of arts in African and African-American studies. She then attended Cornell University Medical School and obtained her medical degree in 1981.

Dr. Jemison was working in West Africa when she learned that NASA was accepting applications for the astronaut corps. She would not let the opportunity to become an astronaut pass her by, so she sent for an application, even though she was a long way from home.

She was back in California and working for a health care organization when the call came in June 1987. She had been accepted, after a series of interviews, into the astronaut corps.

She advises young people: "Define what it is you want to do, define what your idea of your happiness and success is, and not what someone else's is. Then decide what skills you need to obtain that, and then just work for them. And realize there are . . . ups and downs in the road, and what you need to do is to live through the ups and downs and you'll eventually come to it."

Dr. Mae C. Jemison lived through the ups and downs, and for eight days in September 1992, she traveled to space as the science mission specialist on the spaceship *Endeavor*. Her childhood dream became a reality.

Dr. Jemison is the first African-American woman astronaut.

MORE WOMEN OF HOPE

Here are some additional extraordinary African-American women whose lives and accomplishments you will want to learn more about. Some of them are famous, others are little known, unsung heroes. All have overcome obstacles of race and gender, and have by their examples and efforts given us courage and hope. The women represented in this book are but a few of the countless black women who continue to make a difference to their families and their communities.

AVIATOR

BESSIE COLEMAN, c.1893–1926, Aviator. First African-American woman to receive an international pilot's license.

ARTISTS, WRITERS, ETC.

PHILLIS WHEATLEY, c.1753–1784, Poet. First black writer in the United States to publish a book of poetry.

(MARY) EDMONIA LEWIS, c.1843–c.1900, Sculptor. One of the first artists to gain wide acclaim who was of both African-American and Native-American descent.

HATTIE MCDANIEL, c.1898–1952, Actress. First African-American actress to receive an Academy Award.

KATHERINE DUNHAM, 1910–, Dancer, Choreographer, and Anthropologist. Her creative innovations, which included African and Caribbean dance movements, revolutionized modern dance.

JEAN BLACKWELL HUTSON, 1914–1998, Curator and Chief of Schomburg Center for Research in Black Culture from 1948–1980.

GWENDOLYN BROOKS, 1917–, Writer and Poet. First African American to receive a Pulitzer prize, 1950. In 1968, she was named Poet Laureate of Illinois.

LORRAINE HANSBERRY, 1930–1965, Playwright. Her play, the critically acclaimed *A Raisin in the Sun*, was the first theatrical drama written by an African-American woman to be performed on Broadway.

LORNA SIMPSON, 1960–, Photographer and Conceptual Artist. One of the first black women photographers to exhibit her work in major art museums and exhibitions in the United States and abroad.

MUSICIANS

ELIZABETH COTTEN, c.1892–1987, Singer, Guitarist, and Songwriter. She did not begin to perform professionally until she was sixty-seven years old and, in 1984, won a Grammy Award.

MARIAN ANDERSON, 1902–1993, Opera Singer. In 1955, Marian Anderson became the first African American to perform as a soloist at the Metropolitan Opera House in New York City, opening doors for future black soloists.

WILLIE MAE FORD SMITH, 1904–, Gospel Singer. Called the mother of gospel music, in 1988, she received an award from the National Endowment for the Arts for her contributions to gospel.

MAHALIA JACKSON, 1911–1972, Gospel Singer. She has been called one of the world's greatest gospel singers. She contributed her talent to the civil rights movement.

(ZENSI) MIRIAM MAKEBA, 1932–, Singer and Songwriter. She used her incredible voice and talent to protest racial injustice in South Africa, where she was born.

CAREGIVERS

REBECCA J. COLE, 1846–1922, Physician. She was one of the first black women doctors to practice in New

York, Philadelphia, and Washington, D.C. She practiced for fifty years.

SUSIE BAKER KING TAYLOR, 1848–1912, Civil War Nurse and Teacher for the First South Carolina Volunteers.

CLARA MCBRIDE HALE (MOTHER HALE), 1905–1995, Child-Care Innovator. Helped and nurtured hundreds of children whose mothers could not care for them.

JANE COOKE WRIGHT, 1919–, Physician. Professor and specialist in cancer research.

CLARICE WILLS REID, 1931–, Physician. Specialist in sickle-cell anemia research.

EDUCATORS

CHARLOTTE FORTEN GRIMKÉ, 1837–1914, Teacher, Writer, and Abolitionist. She taught in a freedmen's school in South Carolina during the Civil War.

LUCY CRAFT LANEY, 1854–1933, Teacher and Administrator. Lucy Laney was a gifted teacher who devoted her life to her school and her students, preparing many of them for advanced degrees.

MARY MCLEOD BETHUNE, 1875–1955, Teacher and Activist. Founder of the Daytona Normal and Industrial Institute for Negro Girls, today known as the Bethune-Cookman College.

RUBY MIDDLETON FORSYTHE, 1905–1992, Teacher. For over fifty years, Ruby Forsythe taught in a one-room schoolhouse on Pawley's Island, South Carolina.

JOHNNETTA B. COLE, 1936–, Educator and Anthropologist. The first African-American woman president of Spelman College in Atlanta, Georgia.

ACTIVISTS

SOJOURNER TRUTH, c.1797–1883, Activist. An abolitionist orator, she dedicated her life to ending slavery and racism.

MARY CHURCH TERRELL, 1863–1954, Activist. She organized women to speak out for their rights and equal justice for all people.

AUDLEY MOORE (QUEEN MOTHER MOORE), 1898–1997, Activist. Audley Moore was a community organizer in the struggle for equal rights for people of African descent.

ROSA PARKS, 1913–, Activist. She made history when she refused to give up her seat to a white passenger on a city bus in Montgomery, Alabama, in 1955.

DAISY LEE GATSON BATES, c.1920–, Civil Rights Leader and Journalist. Daisy Bates was the driving force behind the fight to desegregate Central High School in Little Rock, Arkansas, in 1957.

CONSTANCE BAKER MOTLEY, 1921–, Federal Judge. After a long and distinguished career as a civil rights lawyer, in 1966, Justice Motley was the first African-American woman to be appointed as a federal judge.

SHIRLEY CHISOLM, 1924–, Legislator. In 1968, she became the first black woman to be elected to Congress and served her Brooklyn district for seven terms.

ANGELA DAVIS, 1944–, Activist and Educator. Her work and life has been dedicated to the struggle against racial oppression and injustice.

ATHLETES

ALTHEA GIBSON, 1927–, Tennis Champion and Professional Golfer. Althea broke racial barriers in tennis and golf, and won at both Wimbledon and the U.S. Open in 1957 and 1958.

WILMA RUDOLPH, 1940–1994, Olympic Champion. Overcoming the effects of childhood polio, in 1960, Wilma Rudolph became the first woman to ever win three gold medals in track.

FLORENCE GRIFFITH JOYNER, 1959–, Olympic Champion. She won three gold medals in track and field in the 1988 Olympics, and was honored as the top amateur athlete in the world that year.

Annotated Bibliography

CHRISTIAN, BARBARA. *Black Women Novelists*. Westport: Greenwood Press, 1980. The novels of Toni Morrison and Alice Walker are included in this in-depth critical analysis of the work of selected black women writers.

DELANY, SARAH AND A. ELIZABETH, WITH AMY HILL HEARTH. *Having Our Say*. New York: Kodansha International, 1993. The Delany sisters narrate the important events of their long lives.

DUSTER, ALFREDA M., ed. *Crusade for Justice: The Autobiography of Ida B. Wells*. Chicago: University of Chicago Press, 1970. Ida B. Wells-Barnett narrates the story of her life.

EDELMAN, MARIAN WRIGHT. *The Measure of Our Success: A Letter to My Children and Yours*. Boston: Beacon Press, 1992. Edelman's moving and profound thoughts on family and children.

ELLIOT, JEFFREY M., ed. *Conversations with Maya Angelou*. Jackson and London: University Press of Mississippi, 1989. A collection of interviews with Maya Angelou.

EVANS, MARI, ed. *Black Women Writers (1950–1980)*. Garden City: Anchor Books, 1984. A collection of essays analyzing the writing of Maya Angelou, Toni Morrison, Alice Walker, and other black women writers.

HARRIS, TRUDIER, ed. *Selected Works of Ida B. Wells-Barnett*. New York and Oxford: Oxford University Press, 1991. A compilation of selected publications, including *A Red Record*, where Wells-Barnett gives actual statistics on the hundreds of lynching incidents from 1892–1894.

HASKINS, JAMES. *Black Theater in America*. New York: HarperCollins Publishers, 1982. Traces the history of African-American theater and includes information on Ruby Dee and her husband, Ossie Davis.

IGUS, TOYOMI, ed. *Book of Black Heroes: Great Women in the Struggle*. Orange, New Jersey: Just Us Books, Inc., 1991. Biographies of 84 African-American women in a variety of professions.

LANKER, BRIAN. *I Dream a World*. New York: Stewart, Tabori & Chang, 1989. Photographs and personal narratives of 75 African-American women.

LERNER, GERDA, ed. *Black Women in White America*. New York: Random House, 1973. The history of black women in America, told through documents and first-person narratives.

WALKER, ALICE. *In Search of Our Mothers' Gardens*. New York: Harcourt Brace Jovanovich, 1983. A collection of essays that gives readers insights into Ms. Walker's heart and mind.